WALKING
in the
CONFIDENCE
of
GOD
in
TROUBLED
TIMES

WALKING
in the
CONFIDENCE
of
GOD
in
TROUBLED
TIMES

DR. CREFLO A.
DOLLAR

WARNER
Faith®

NEW YORK BOSTON NASHVILLE

Unless otherwise indicated, all Scripture quotations are taken from the *King James Version* of the Bible.

Scripture quotations marked (NIV) are taken from *The Holy Bible: New International Version*® NIV®. Copyright © 1973, 1978, 1984 by International Bible Society. Used by permission of Zondervan Publishing House. All rights reserved.

Scripture quotations marked (AMP) are taken from *The Amplified Bible*. *Old Testament* copyright © 1965, 1987 by the Zondervan Corporation, Grand Rapids, Michigan. *New Testament* copyright © 1958, 1987 by The Lockman Foundation, La Habra, California. Used by permission.

Warner Books Edition
Copyright © 2000, 2004, 2006 by Dr. Creflo A. Dollar
Creflo Dollar Ministries
2500 Burdette Road
College Park, GA 30349
All rights reserved.

Warner Faith

Time Warner Book Group
1271 Avenue of the Americas, New York, NY 10020
Visit our Web site at www.twbookmark.com.

Warner Faith® and the Warner Faith logo are trademarks of Time Warner Book Group Inc.

Printed in the United States of America

First Warner Faith Edition: March 2006
10 9 8 7 6 5 4 3 2 1

LCCN: 2005937680
ISBN-13: 978-0-446-69839-9
ISBN: 0-446-69839-3

Contents

Confidence: The Missing Substance of Faith

The Missing Ingredient

Do you get results every time you pray? Are you experiencing the full manifestation of God's promises of healing, provision and deliverance in your daily life?

For most believers, the answer to these questions is a frustrated "no." In fact, for too many, prayer is more like a roll of the dice than an exercise in faith. Other times it may seem like the show *Let's Make a Deal!*, in which Christians try to bargain with God in an attempt to get Him to move on their behalf. Still other believers resort to asking for signs (omens, proof or hard evidence) in an attempt to gain some assurance that God will meet their needs before they fully believe the Word of God.

You probably recognize yourself in one of the above examples. I think we've all been there at one time or another in our lives. I don't need to tell you that all of the straining and striving to get God to move on your behalf can be a disheartening experience. However, I've got news for you. Not only does that kind of prayer not work very well, it's totally unnecessary!

God never intended for His children to beg, plead or bargain for His promises to be fulfilled in their lives. His earnest desire is that you experience abundant life—the full manifestation of every promise in His Word. That means total provision, prosperity, absolute health, well-being and deliverance from all oppression.

So why aren't most Christians, despite all of their confessing and believing, experiencing that kind of life? Why do we still bombard heaven with "roll the dice" prayers and "let's make a deal" petitions? The answer is profoundly simple. Each of the aforementioned methods of prayer has a common missing element. They lack the one key component that will energize your faith and revolutionize your prayer life. That missing ingredient is *confidence*.

What Is Confidence?

Confidence means, "assurance; complete and total persuasion." It also closely parallels the meaning of "trust." When you trust something, you have confidence in it. For example, when it rains, I open my umbrella, *confident* in the fact that it will shield me from the rain. There is no doubt in my mind that that umbrella will keep me dry; I *trust* its ability to do that. Confidence is the quality which enables you to endure and overcome adversity. It causes you to undertake a difficult task with diligence. You'll never take a firm stand for something without first having confidence.

Another term closely identified with confidence is "boldness." In fact, boldness can often be used interchangeably with confidence when talking about spiritual principles. That's because, in Scripture, both words are derived from the same Greek root word. Don't get the wrong idea, however. Many of us have a distorted concept of what boldness is. We tend to think it means seeing how loud you can talk or how belligerent you can be. That's not boldness—that's your flesh.

Finally, boldness is intricately tied to the concepts of "yieldedness" and "obedience." There can be no true obedience where there is no confidence. Nor can you yield yourself to someone whom you don't trust. Your confidence is the ingredient that makes your faith work. It might be the missing piece to your faith puzzle.

Study Questions

1. What is God's earnest desire for your life?

_____

_____

_____

_____

_____

2. Why does it matter whether we pray with confidence or not?

_____

_____

_____

_____

3. What can you do today to build the kind of confidence that will energize your faith and revolutionize your prayer life?

_____

_____

_____

_____

_____

My prayer in the confidence of God's Word . . .

_____

_____

_____

_____

_____

_____

_____

2

The Power of Confidence

PEOPLE HAVE SAID to me, "Brother Dollar, I know I have faith, yet my faith doesn't seem to be producing anything." This is a complaint I've heard too many times to count. If you can identify with that statement, take comfort in knowing that there's probably nothing wrong with your faith. You may simply be lacking the vital ingredient of confidence.

Confidence is the force that launches your faith. It propels faith forward just like rocket boosters send a space shuttle into orbit. Trying to operate your faith without the force of confidence is like trying to take off in an airplane that has no engines. There's probably nothing wrong with the overall structural integrity of the plane; it's simply missing a crucial element.

Some people might say, "Brother Dollar, I've confessed prosperity scriptures over and over, and my bills still aren't getting paid." You can quote scriptures until you're hoarse, but if confidence doesn't rise up and propel your faith, you won't receive the manifestation of your confessions. Speaking words of faith is not enough; even acting on those words is not enough. You must have confidence in those words for them to have the power to change your circumstances; and that comes only through meditating the Word of God until it becomes more real to you than your situation or circumstance. This is called establishing your heart in the Word of God.

Think of it this way: Have you ever seen a mother take her small child to the bus stop and put him on the school bus? It is confidence that allows the mother to put her child on the bus and walk away. Confidence is like a mother. It takes faith by the hand, leads it to a "bus stop" in your life, and sends it on its way to reach its desired destination. It is the force that energizes and activates your words.

Just because you open your mouth and say something doesn't mean those words are full of confidence. Many Christians make empty confessions thinking that repeatedly saying the same things will get results; it becomes a religious activity with no power behind it.

Only when your heart is established in the Word of God will confidence rise from within you. The difference between speaking empty words and words that are backed by the force of faith will be apparent by the results that you get. For example, imagine that there are two singers standing in front of a crowd. The first singer squeaks out a song in a weak, trembling voice. Then the second singer performs the same song and gives a commanding performance, belting out the song with enthusiasm. What is the difference between the two? One singer sings with confidence, while the other one isn't as convinced of his talent. The confident singer will make an impact on his audience while the other singer's listeners will pick up on his timidity.

Fill Up Your Words

Don't misunderstand. Words are important; however, alone they cannot change your circumstances. They are simply spiritual containers, and what you fill them with is what makes the difference.

Imagine an empty glass beside a pitcher of water. In order for the glass to become full of water, some outside force has to move the pitcher and pour the water into the glass. Confidence can be likened to that force which pours the water from the pitcher (faith that comes by hearing the Word of God) into the glass (your words). Simply put, confidence pours faith into your words, and then your faith-filled words go into action when spoken!

The missing link in many believers' spiritual lives is confidence. They have faith. They have the corresponding action that must accompany faith. However, what they've lacked is the force of confidence to get the whole process moving. We've wanted the water in the glass but we have not been able to get it from the pitcher into the glass because we haven't understood the importance of confidence.

It Ain't Over 'Til It's Over

What does confidence look like? A good example can be found in Habakkuk 3:17–18: "*Although the fig tree shall not blossom, neither shall fruit be in the vines; the labour of the olive shall fail, and the fields shall yield no meat; the flock shall be cut off from the fold, and there shall be no herd in the stalls: Yet I will rejoice in the Lord, I will joy in the God of my salvation.*"

Now here's a man with confidence! His crops have failed; his livestock has been destroyed; nothing is going right for him. Yet how does he respond to his circumstances? He says, "I will rejoice in the Lord." Why is he so optimistic in the face of such adversity? Verse 19 says, "*The Lord God is my strength, and he will make my feet like hinds' feet, and he will make me to walk upon mine high places. . . .*" This person had a revelation of God's love for Him in spite of His circumstances and it boosted his confidence in God's delivering power.

Remember, it's not over until it's over—someone has to win. Will it be you or the devil? You can't just quit because of the circumstances that you may face. Like Habakkuk, you must hold on to your confidence no matter what the situation looks like. You must *know*—even though the light bill is due, the phone company is threatening to disconnect you and your next paycheck is a week away—that the Lord will bring you through. You must make Him your confidence.

Study Questions

1. What gives words the power to change your circumstances?

_____

_____

_____

_____

_____

2. Have you ever prayed for something and felt like your prayers went unanswered? What do you think was really going on?

_____

_____

_____

_____

3. How can Habakkuk 3:17–18 inspire you to pray with confidence?

_____

_____

_____

_____

My prayer in the confidence of God's Word . . .

_____

_____

_____

_____

_____

_____

_____

3

Understanding the Force of Confidence

WHEN YOU'RE FULL of confidence, you know "in your knower" that God's Word is going to produce exactly what it says It will, no matter how bad the present circumstances may seem.

How do you develop that kind of confidence? Before you can begin to cultivate the kind of unshakeable confidence that will move your faith to new heights, you must first have a greater biblical understanding of what it is and how it works.

Fully Persuaded

When you think of confidence, think about a person who is fully persuaded. This person can't be moved from his or her stance. A perfect example of a confident person is Abraham: *"And [Abraham] being fully persuaded that, what he had promised, he was able also to perform"* (Romans 4:21).

Abraham was 100 years old and his wife Sarah was 90 when the Lord told them that He would bless them with a son and make their descendants outnumber the stars. Of course, Abraham and Sarah didn't reach the point of being fully persuaded right away. In fact, when God's promise seemed a little slow in coming, they decided to help Him out.

Sarah arranged for her personal servant, Hagar, to have sexual intercourse with Abraham. The result was a son—Ishmael. However, that was not what God had promised. The barren Sarah was the one who, along with Abraham, would bear a child whose seed would bless all nations of the earth. That couldn't happen, however, until Abraham got to the point of being fully persuaded, or completely confident.

This is where most of us miss it. We never become fully persuaded that God will do what He has promised in His Word. We read a promise in Scripture, and then timidly tiptoe into a confession or action that is supposed to resemble faith. The problem is that everything we say and do lacks confidence. It's like hiring an employee to do a job that he is reluctant to do. It shows up in the quality of his work. He may go through all the motions, but if his heart isn't in it, the quality of work will be sub-par and he won't be willing to put forth any extra effort to get the job done. He does just enough to stay employed.

Ultimately, Abraham became absolutely, totally convinced that God was faithful to keep His promises. He reached the point of being fully persuaded. Another way of saying it is that he had "blessed assurance." When you receive blessed assurance, you get an empowerment that comes only from God. It's a supernatural conviction that what God has promised will indeed come to pass. It was only when Abraham reached that point that the promise of God could manifest in the natural realm. The same is true for you. You'll never see the miraculous manifestations of God's promises in your life until you reach the point of having fully persuaded faith.

Hold on Tight!

Once you've developed confidence in a promise of God, the next thing you have to do is hold on to it with everything you've got. Hebrews 3:6, 14 says, *"But Christ as a son over his own house; whose house are we, if we hold fast the confidence and the rejoicing of the hope firm unto the end. . . . For we are made partakers of Christ, if we hold the beginning of our confidence stedfast unto the end."*

If you want to receive the promises of God in your life, you must hold on tightly to your confidence until the end. When is the end? When you have the manifestation of the promise in which you have placed your confidence. Never let go of your confidence until you've received your miracle.

Don't think for a minute that holding on to your confidence is going to be easy. If you're standing on a promise from God's Word, the devil is going to pull out every trick in his bag to try to get you to waver in your confidence. He'll use well-meaning family members, friends, television and any other medium at his disposal to try to shake your faith in God's promise. If you're believing God for healing, hold fast until your healing manifests. If you're trusting God's Word concerning finances, hang on with a steely grip until your situation turns around. Hold on, no matter how long it takes.

Look at verse 14 again: *". . . if we hold the beginning of our confidence stedfast unto the end."* This scripture tells us that confidence has a beginning and an end. Often the beginning of confidence comes when we sow seeds. If you need money, sow financial seeds. Sow your seed into good soil and sow it in confidence. If you need healing, sow seeds by praying for the sick. Sow your seeds in confidence that they will produce a hundredfold return. Confidence begins with sowing.

A confident beginning is not "hoping and praying." You can't sow seeds *hoping* that you will see a return. There is no confidence in that. If God said it, He will do it. He cannot lie. He framed the entire universe with the power and integrity of His Word. If He told one lie, everything in existence would disintegrate. Begin every journey of faith with confidence and hold on to it until the end.

Claim Your Reward

Satan is determined to have you lose your confidence because he hates you and doesn't want you to receive your reward from God. That's right! Confidence always produces a reward.

Hebrews 10:35 says, *"Cast not away therefore your confidence, which hath great recompence of reward."*

Don't cast away (throw away, toss aside, let go of) your confidence. It's just what the devil wants you to do. In fact, he knows that if he can destroy your confidence in God's faithfulness and in His Word, you're finished. Be on guard. The enemy won't come in and try to wipe out your confidence all at once; instead, he'll try to erode it away a little bit at a time: a little word of discouragement spoken here, a little bad news there. If you're not careful, you'll eventually find your confidence collapsing around you like a house of cards. So don't cast away your confidence. Hang on and claim your reward.

Confidence Is Your Foundation and Strength

Proverbs 3:26 says, *"For the Lord shall be thy confidence, and shall keep thy foot from being taken."* Having the Lord as your confidence will keep your foot from stumbling. In other words, when you trust Him, you'll be able to stand in the midst of adversity. You'll be able to walk securely on your path in life knowing that God is backing you up.

When you're standing immovable on God's Word, you're in a position to receive great blessings. The devil will try to move you from your stance; however, when you make the Lord your confidence, you can be assured that your foot will remain firm.

When you're fighting the good fight of faith, it is crucial

that you have sufficient strength for the battle. Spiritual strength can mean the difference between prosperity and poverty, deliverance and oppression, sickness and health, even life and death.

How do you gain spiritual strength? According to Isaiah 30:15, you gain spiritual strength through confidence: *"For thus saith the Lord God, the Holy One of Israel; In returning and rest shall ye be saved; in quietness and in confidence shall be your strength. . . ."*

The strength that comes through confidence will get you into the Word when you think you're too tired to study. It will get you up for a time of fellowship with God when your flesh would rather stay in bed. It will get you to church to be fed the Word when your body is demanding to relax on the couch. Confidence is the strength of your faith.

Pray with Confidence

Prayer doesn't accomplish much until it's energized by the force of confidence. There is nothing quite as powerful as a prayer that you *know* is going to come to pass. How does that kind of faith come about? It's simple. First, it comes through confidence that God hears you when you pray. First John 5:14–15 (NIV) says, *"This is the confidence we have in approaching God: that if we ask anything according to his will, he hears us. And if we know that he hears us—whatever we ask—we know that we have what we asked of him."*

Second, you must be confident that you're praying in accordance with the will of God; you do that by praying the Word. Faith comes when the will of God is known and God's Word is His will. Find a promise in the Bible that speaks about your particular situation, and then pray it and stand on it. You'll know that you're praying God's will because you're praying His Word.

Third, as a result of doing the first two steps, you must have confidence that you have that for which you pray. When you pray with confidence, things happen.

Study Questions

1. How does the story of Abraham and Sarah impact your confidence in God's promises?

_____

_____

_____

_____

_____

2. How will you stand strong against the Enemy the next time he tries to steal your confidence?

_____

_____

_____

_____

3. What biblical promise will you stand on to pray confidently about your situation?

_____

_____

_____

_____

My prayer in the confidence of God's Word . . .

_____

_____

_____

_____

_____

_____

_____

Love: A Confidence Booster

It HAS BEEN established that confidence is the missing substance of faith, but you may be wondering why. The reason is that confidence is what connects you to God's power, or anointing. The anointing is His ability to remove people's burdens and destroy their yokes. It is responsible for canceling your debt, healing your body and setting you free from oppression. Without confidence operating in your life, you can't tap into this power.

Do you remember what it was like growing up? For most of us, when our parents said they were going to do something for us, they made sure they did it one way or another. We didn't doubt the fact that there would be something on the table to eat. We knew they would somehow come through for us because we had confidence in their love for us. In the same way, you simply have to believe in God's ability *and* willingness to get involved in your situation and express His love on your behalf.

Look at 2 Corinthians 2:14, which says, *"Now thanks be unto God, which always causes us to triumph in Christ, and maketh manifest the savour of his knowledge by us in every place."* The anointing of might is responsible for "always causing us to triumph." It is the ability to do anything. Every scripture is a promise and guarantee straight from heaven. God is the One who gives you the victory, but do you believe it?

This anointing we've been talking about resides in you through Jesus; you are more than a conqueror through Him (Romans 8:37). Psalm 24:8 even lets you know just how strong He is when it says, *"Who is the King of glory? The Lord strong and mighty, the Lord mighty in battle"* (AMP). Ephesians 6:10 also says, *"Finally, my brethren, be strong in the Lord, and in the power of his might."* Clearly, God's might is His power manifested; nothing can stand against it and succeed. That very power resides in you! When you have confidence in *His* ability and not your own, your faith is strengthened.

Activating this power comes through two avenues: 1) having revelation knowledge from God's Word, and 2) confidence. The revelation knowledge that God wants you to have is of His love for you. When you know He loves you, your confidence in His desire to help you becomes strong.

Getting this type of confidence-boosting revelation comes only through spending quality time with Him in His Word until He speaks to you about your particular situation. While the written Word of God is the starting point for revelation, it isn't until you are able to *hear* God's voice on the matter, spoken directly to your spirit that your confidence will soar to new heights.

God loves you. That's the bottom line. You may have confidence in His *ability* to come through for you, but do you really believe that He *will*? Believing in His willingness to get involved in your situation is what will enable you to experience breakthrough.

Mark 11:23–24 says, *"For verily I say unto you, That whosoever shall say unto this mountain, Be thou removed, and be thou cast into the sea; and shall not doubt in his heart, but shall believe that those things which he saith shall come to pass; he shall have whatsoever he saith. Therefore I say unto you, What things soever ye desire, when ye pray, believe that ye receive them, and ye shall have them."* Make no mistake about it, your loving Father wants to bless you, but you have to believe it in order for it to become a reality.

Understanding Love's Love

In order to have confidence in God, you have to understand and believe His love for you. God doesn't just have love, He *is* love. First John 4:16 says, *"And we have known and believed the love that God hath to us. God is love; and he that dwelleth in love dwelleth in God, and God in him."* God desires to bless you! It's all He knows how to do because love is His nature. You have to know in your heart that He loves you and refuse to accept anything else the devil tries to throw at you.

So, do you believe the Love? That is a question that only you can answer. When you walk around in condemnation, doubt and unbelief, you don't believe in His Love and your confidence in Him is undermined. Your heavenly Father wants to do you good, give you the desires of your heart and fulfill your needs. He wants to fight on your behalf and display His might so that you can emerge victorious in every situation and circumstance you face.

Be confident that nothing can separate you from God's love (Romans 8:35–39). If you believe that He loves you, then you know that anything He has promised you in His Word and spoken to your heart that lines up with His Word He will perform for you.

The Scriptures are full of references to God and His mercy. In fact, the Bible is a collection of love letters filled with His promises to you. Phrases like *tender mercy, loving kindness, truth* and *faithfulness* describe His character. He isn't waiting to strike you with a lightning bolt when you mess up, but He does want to bless you in every possible way. However, you have to believe the love.

Since your understanding of God's love will be the key factor in the confidence connection, it is essential to grasp the type of love with which God loves you and the way He expects you to love Him. The God-kind of love is called *agape* love. It isn't emotional human love, but is unconditional love that continues to operate even when it is done wrong (1 Corinthians 13). That is the kind of love with which the Father loves you, and He wants you to direct this type of love towards others. At the same time, to *agapeo* God means that you bind yourself to Him, and become one with Him. In other words, your purposes, plans, pursuits and agenda align with His; you become consumed with your relationship with Him and His Word.

Developing in this type of love will boost your confidence and strengthen your faith in God. Knowing Him as Love will open the floodgates of might to cause you to be victorious in every situation and circumstance that you face. With Love backing you up, the devil will have to back down.

Study Questions

1. When have you seen God's power and presence in your life?

_____

_____

_____

_____

_____

2. How does God's love inspire you to love Him and others more?

_____

_____

_____

_____

_____

3. God is the One Who gives you the victory. Do you believe it?

_____

_____

_____

_____

_____

My prayer in the confidence of God's Word . . .

_____

_____

_____

_____

_____

_____

_____

5

Developing Confidence

So far, we've seen that confidence is the missing link in the chain of faith—the force that launches faith into motion. It's the trigger that enables your faith to work the same way every time. That's important, because God wants you to know exactly how to obtain healing, get your bills paid or get whatever else you need, and get it every time.

Now that you're excited and ready to get your prayers answered, you might ask, "Okay, I'm convinced, Brother Dollar. I need and want confidence. How do I get it?" That's a fair question. The answer is in the Word of God. Let's look at some scriptural conditions and steps to develop the force of confidence in your life.

A Heart That Is True

If you want to deal with God and His Word with full assurance, or confidence, you must first have a "true heart." Hebrews 10:22–23 says: *"Let us draw near with a true heart in full assurance of faith, having our hearts sprinkled from an evil conscience, and our bodies washed with pure water. Let us hold fast the profession of our faith without wavering; (for he is faithful that promised)."* Don't try to lie to God or manipulate Him; instead, say, "Lord, I have sinned today." In doing so, you operate with a true heart. That level of honesty and transparency is a beautiful thing to God. The result? You are able to draw near to him "in full assurance of faith."

What is the full assurance of faith? Confident faith. Don't come to God with faith alone; come with confidence, too. Have confidence in God's goodness, in the Word, in His grace to cleanse you from all unrighteousness, in your position in Christ Jesus and in the faith life. A true heart is a prerequisite to that kind of confidence.

What other people know about you is not as important as what you know about yourself and what God knows about you. When you know that there is sin in your life and your heart is accusing you and making you feel guilty and condemned, it becomes very difficult to have confidence in God answering your prayers. First John 3:20–22 (AMP) says:

> . . . *Whenever our hearts in [tormenting] self-accusation make us feel guilty and condemn us. [For we are in God's hands.] For He is above and greater than our consciences (our hearts), and He knows (perceives and understands) everything [nothing is hidden from Him]. And, beloved, if our consciences (our hearts) do not accuse us [if they do not make us feel guilty and condemn us], we have confidence (complete assurance and boldness) before God, And we receive from Him whatever we ask.*

Keeping your heart intact by refusing to get into condemnation and guilt is extremely important if you are to have confidence toward God.

Conceive Your Miracle

Are you beginning to grasp the relationship between confidence and faith? Do you see why it's pointless to confess "by His stripes I am healed" when you have no confidence in those words? Your words are only empty containers. It takes both confidence and faith to produce results in your life.

One day as I was meditating on the correlation between faith and confidence, the Spirit of God spoke to me and said, "They are mating." This surprised me at first, but as I thought about it some more, I began to understand the truth of what He was saying.

A woman can't have a baby alone. Nor can a man have one without a woman. It takes both to create offspring. The same is true with faith and confidence. When they come together, the thing that you are believing God for is conceived. Hold on to that confidence long enough and it will be birthed in the natural realm. At that point, you'll see the physical manifestation of that which was conceived in the spirit—your miracle.

The Tradition Trap

As we have seen, the Word of God is a powerful thing. Yet there is something that can stop it from operating effectively for you—religious tradition.

Jesus once told a religious crowd that their traditions had rendered the Word of God ineffective (Mark 7:13). Many believers have been taught through the religious traditions of various denominations that God doesn't work wonders anymore. "The age of miracles has passed," they're told. As a result, they have no confidence in God's promises of miraculous deliverance, healing and provision. Many others have attended churches in which they have seen some level of manifestation. They've seen great men of power and anointed ministers; however, they have no confidence that what they've seen can ever be a reality in their own personal lives. They simply go through the motions without seeing any real results. This reinforces their lack of confidence. It's a downward spiral of despair and frustration.

The good news is that the cycle works the other way, too! When you hear the Word of God and really begin to understand it, confidence and faith will begin to rise up in your spirit. You'll step out and believe God for a little miracle. For example, perhaps you need some food, and by faith you receive what you need. Then, when you need a bill paid and you don't have any money left, you'll remember how the Word worked when you needed a meal. More faith and confidence will rise up within you. Together the two will go to work, and your need will be miraculously met. It's an upward cycle of ever-increasing faith, confidence and power.

Expect Opposition

Operating in confidence does not mean that you will not encounter adversity. In 1 Thessalonians 2:2, the apostle Paul said, ". . . *But even after that we had suffered before, and were shamefully entreated, as ye know, at Philippi, we were bold in our God to speak unto you the gospel of God with much contention.*" If you plan to reap the rewards of walking in confidence and boldness, you'd better get ready for some contention. Just as with Paul, controversy, contention and opposition tend to follow a person of true boldness. Therefore, it's vital that you learn how to hold on to your confidence in the midst of such resistance.

The three Hebrew boys—Shadrach, Meshach and Abednego—that Nebuchadnezzar threw into the fiery furnace are great examples of confidence under pressure. Their response to his death threat was, *"If it be so, our God whom we serve is able to deliver us from the burning fiery furnace, and he will deliver us out of thine hand, O king"* (Daniel 3:17). Can you hear their confidence? "We don't care what you do to us. We are not going to bow down and worship your idols. We are fully persuaded that our God is able to deliver us!"

Daniel is another great example. His boldness in prayer caused contention. As a result he ended up in a dungeon full of hungry lions. If most of us found ourselves in a lions' den, we'd be lunch! But Daniel's quiet confidence put his faith in motion. Faith brought angels in on the scene to shut the watering mouths of those lions (Daniel 6:10–22).

Why does contention always follow bold believers? It is designed by Satan to destroy their confidence. He knows that if he can take away your calm assurance through trouble, strife and opposition, then your faith will lose the jets that put it into flight. Hold on to your confidence in the face of contention. If you do, you will come out on top just as surely as Paul, Daniel and those three Hebrew boys did.

Study Questions

1. What does it mean to have a "true heart"?

_____

_____

_____

_____

_____

2. How are faith and confidence like a husband and wife?

_____

_____

_____

_____

_____

3. What Scriptures will you hold on to when opposition comes your way?

_____

_____

_____

_____

_____

My prayer in the confidence of God's Word . . .

_____

_____

_____

_____

_____

_____

_____

6

You Can Walk in Confidence

CONFIDENCE, THE KIND of boldness that puts your faith into motion, is really not a complicated thing to develop. You don't have to be extremely intelligent, sophisticated or refined to have it. No matter who you are, you can have mountain-moving confidence. How? You receive it the same way a couple of simple fishermen from Galilee did: *"Now when they saw the boldness of Peter and John, and perceived that they were unlearned and ignorant men, they marvelled; and they took knowledge of them, that they had been with Jesus"* (Acts 4:13).

Peter and John had boldness that could not only be heard, but could also be seen! How do you get confidence like that? By spending time with Jesus. Spend time with Him in prayer. Fellowship with Him in worship. Get to know Him in His Word. Show me a person who is fully persuaded, and I'll show you a person who has been with Jesus.

Ask and You Shall Receive

Ultimately, the most powerful key to developing confidence is the simplest one of all: Ask for it! Acts 4 continues: *"And now, Lord, behold their threatenings: and grant unto thy servants, that with all boldness they may speak thy word. . . . And when they [the disciples] had prayed, the place was shaken where they were assembled together; and they were all filled with the Holy Ghost, and they spake the word of God with boldness"* (vv. 29, 31). When the New Testament church was faced with opposition, they came together and prayed for boldness. They prayed and they were filled. It was as simple as that.

Nothing produces confidence in you like being filled with the Holy Spirit, Who is yours for the asking. Luke 11:13 says, *"If ye then, being evil, know how to give good gifts unto your children: how much more shall your heavenly Father give the Holy Spirit to them that ask him?"*

You don't ever have to be without confidence again. Imagine never again praying without knowing that your prayer was heard and answered. Imagine never again laying hands on someone without knowing that power would flow out of you to touch that person's body. Imagine never tithing or giving without knowing that you were going to receive a hundredfold return.

All of that, and much more, is possible when you unleash the force of confidence and join it to your faith.

Study Questions

1. How can you develop confidence like Jesus' disciples had?

_____

_____

_____

_____

_____

2. What is the most powerful key to developing confidence?

_____

_____

_____

_____

_____

3. How will your life be different when you unleash the force of confidence and join it to your faith?

_____

_____

_____

_____

_____

My prayer in the confidence of God's Word . . .

_____

_____

_____

_____

_____

_____

_____

Five Steps to Complete Salvation

1. Recognize and admit that you are a sinner (Psalm 51:5).

2. Repent of your sins (1 John 1:9).

3. Confess Jesus Christ as your Lord and Savior (Romans 10:9–10).

   "Father, in the name of Jesus, I recognize and admit that I am a sinner. I repent of my sins, making a 180–degree turn away from them toward You by changing my heart, mind and direction. I confess with my mouth that Jesus is Lord, and I believe in my heart that You raised Him from the dead. I invite You to come into my life, Lord Jesus, and I thank You that I am saved. Amen."

4. Receive baptism by water (Matthew 3:6) and the Baptism of the Holy Spirit with the evidence of speaking in tongues (Acts 2:3–4, 38; Acts 8:14–17).

5. Pray, read and obey the Word of God daily (Joshua 1:8; Proverbs 4:20–23; 1 John 5:3).

Keys to Receiving the Baptism of the Holy Spirit

1. Understand that the Holy Spirit was poured out on the day of Pentecost (Acts 2:1–4).

2. Remember that salvation is the only qualification necessary for receiving the Baptism of the Holy Spirit (Acts 2:38).

3. Know that the laying on of hands is scriptural (Acts 8:17; Acts 19:6).

4. Dispel all fears about receiving a counterfeit spirit (Luke 11:11–13).

5. Open your mouth as an act of faith to receive the Holy Spirit (Ephesians 5:18–19).

*Walking in the Confidence of
God in Troubled Times*

Introduction:
Living in the Overflow

Early in my ministry, I discovered that although I was constantly studying, teaching, and preaching the Word, something was disturbing my peace. I was spending time in the Word while preparing sermons and ministering, but I was still troubled. I began to notice that certain reports would "get to me"; they would stay in my spirit and bother me. I knew I felt a little drained every time I finished preaching and ministering the Word, but I thought it was just normal fatigue; nothing that a good night's sleep wouldn't cure. Yet I would go to bed and be unable to sleep because my peace would not come back.

I found that things which normally would not have bothered me started absolutely nagging the life out of me to the point that I found myself just trying to keep from going under. I'd pray, "Oh, God, what is wrong with me? Why can't I handle this? After all, I handled it last year. Why not now?"

I got so depressed that I finally said to God, "I don't feel like I can take this anymore. I'm tired of this. I quit." I was in such distress that I felt as if I were dying inside, as if I were crumbling away. I didn't know what to do to fight the problem, because I didn't understand what was wrong.

The Lord finally got my attention and showed me what was happening. He said, *Son, when these problems came to you before, they found no room to occupy because you were filled with My Word. However, as you continue to pour out in preaching, teaching, and ministering, you're forgetting to pour in. You're forgetting to replenish what you've poured out. When you poured out My Word and did not pour anything back in, you left that space unoccupied. That is just what the Devil has been waiting for: some unoccupied space to fill so he can occupy your thinking with bad reports, fear, and worry. You don't have the ability in the natural to combat these things. That is why I have given you My Word; it is a shield to quench the fiery darts of the wicked one.*

I finally began to understand what He meant. I had been down so far that I didn't want to live anymore. I had been trying to figure out where this deep depression was coming from. Suddenly I saw that Satan had been trying to get a foothold in me for months and even years.

The Devil is not stupid! When he finally sees an open door in the life of a born-again Christian who has given him a headache for years, he will take advantage of the opportunity. He will come in and attack with heavy artillery. He will bring in everything he can at one time and attempt to wipe out that Christian!

An Ounce of Prevention

"All right, God," I said, "I see this is my fault. I see where I messed up. I see what happened. Please tell me what to do so I can correct the situation and prevent it from happening again."

What the Lord showed me is not at all that spectacular. It will not make you do flips or dance in the street when you read it. Believe me when I say, however, that it works!

God gave me a simple illustration that I will never forget. He showed me that if you want to remove something from a container of water, an effective way to do so is to create an overflow: to fill the container with water until it overflows. God said to me, *Get in the Word until it creates an overflow.*

He told me that if I would get into His Word and confess it three times a day, my heart would not only be filled with it, but it would begin to overflow with it. Then, when the overflow begins, the current of that flow would wash out the negative thoughts that had been able to enter my heart through my eyes and ears. Finally, the overflow would remove the worry, and only the confidence of God would continue to stay within the circulation of the overflow.

Then God said, *When you are in the overflow, remain there. Live in the overflow.*

Where Did the Trouble Go?

You and I must live in the overflow and minister out of the overflow in order to walk in the confidence of God. When we do, the good material occupying our spirits will not get used up. That good material is what Paul refers to in Philippians 4:8:

> Finally, brethren, whatsoever things are true, whatsoever things are honest, whatsoever things are just, whatsoever things are pure, whatsoever things are lovely, whatsoever things are of good report; if there be any virtue, and if there be any praise, think on these things.

When we fill our spirits with the good material of the Word to the point of overflowing, we prevent the world's troubles and the Devil's lies from getting in and getting to us. When we live in the overflow, we have so much Word occupying the space in our hearts that we leave no room for Satan. In addition, we have enough Word left over to minister to others without being constantly depleted ourselves.

When you get yourself filled to overflowing with the Word, all of a sudden you will wonder what in the world happened to all that trouble you thought you were in! It is amazing how problems shrink in the presence of God and His Word. When you are living in the overflow of God's Word, problems have no space to occupy.

Introduction: Living in the Overflow

Living in the overflow is what enables us to walk in the confidence of God. However, we do not instantaneously overcome problems. Trouble won't necessarily disappear the minute you start filling yourself with God's Word, or even the minute you start living in the overflow. There is always a period of time between "I believe I receive . . ." and "Thank You, Lord! There it is!" There is a space between the faith that says, "I'm healed" or "I'm delivered," and the physical manifestation of your healing or deliverance.

That space between faith and the answer is usually occupied with tribulation, tests, and trials. Like a defensive line in a football game, trouble often seems to block our way to the answer. Trouble's job is to keep us from scoring. Faith's job is to keep us in the game, to keep us pressing toward the end zone, where the promises of God await us. Our job is to get in the Word and find out what we must do to get past that tribulation and into the answer.

In the pages that follow, I want to show you some powerful tactics that you can use to overcome trouble every time it shows up. As you diligently apply the principles of this message, you will find yourself walking in the confidence of God, even in troubled times.

God Is in Control

WE LIVE IN troubled times. I doubt anyone would argue with me about that. A glance at a newspaper or a television newscast should convince anyone that if any day qualifies as the time Jesus foretold in Matthew 24, our day does. The events Jesus said would be signs of His coming and of the end of the world seem to be occurring all around us. He said:

> Take heed that no man deceive you. For many shall come in my name, saying, I am Christ; and shall deceive many. And you shall hear of wars and rumours of wars: see that ye be not troubled: for all these things must come to pass, but the end is not yet. For nation shall rise against nation, and kingdom against kingdom: and there shall be famines, and pestilences, and

earthquakes, in divers places. All these are the begin-
ning of sorrows.

Then shall they deliver you up to be afflicted, and
shall kill you: and ye shall be hated of all nations for my
name's sake. And then shall many be offended, and
shall betray one another, and shall hate one another.

And many false prophets shall rise, and shall deceive
many. And because iniquity shall abound, the love of
many shall wax cold. But he that shall endure unto the
end, the same shall be saved. And this Gospel of the
kingdom shall be preached in all the world for a witness
unto all nations; and then shall the end come.

MATTHEW 24:4–14

Wars, rumors of wars, famines, pestilences, earthquakes,
persecutions, afflictions—we've seen all of these terrible manifestations of tribulation in our own day. However, right in the
middle of this catalog of troubles, Jesus said, "See that ye be
not troubled." Jesus was saying, "In the midst of all this trouble, you can have peace. Trouble will come, but you don't have
to let it trouble you."

Remember One Thing

I know you may be shaking your head and asking, "But how
can I help being troubled with all this going on around me? All
this fear and anxiety and worry are kind of contagious. I know

I shouldn't be anxious, but sometimes it seems like I just can't help it!"

You can keep your peace and walk in fearless confidence even in the midst of these troubled times if you remember one thing: *God is in control.* God is in control of your marriage, your family, your finances, your job, and every aspect of your life. God is even in control over the Devil who is troubling you.

Make no mistake about it. The earth, and the fullness thereof, is still the Lord's. (Ps. 24:1.) The silver and gold belong to the Lord. (Hag. 2:8.) The Devil is the god over the world system, but God is still God over heaven and earth, and He is about to show you and the rest of this world that He is *still* in control.

God is the One who will decide when the end of the world will come. Certainly there is trouble in the world, but there always has been. Jesus said that " 'this Gospel of the kingdom shall be preached' " despite any trouble that might occur in the end times.

The Gospel of Jesus Christ, the Good News, will not roll over and quit just because trouble shows up. "The gospel of this kingdom shall be preached." No matter what problems arise in this last day—whether in the economic system, in the capitals of all the nations of the world, or in the United Nations—nothing can stop the Gospel of Jesus Christ from being preached.

In the middle of trouble, you can be confident in the Good News of the Lord Jesus Christ. You will always have an option either to be troubled or not to be troubled, but this Good News will remain!

The Good News Will Remain

In order to walk in the confidence of God in troubled times, you have to know what the Good News means for you personally. You must find out who you are in Christ and what has been made available to you in your position as a born-again child of God.

Becoming born again is what happened to your spirit after you repented, confessed with your mouth the Lord Jesus Christ, and believed in your heart that God raised Him from the dead. To be born again means to move from darkness into light. Therefore, being born again involves a transition, or translation, from one point to another point, from one position to another position, based on a decision that you make.

However, salvation is what is available to you when you become born again. The word *salvation* in the New Testament comes from the Greek word *soteria*, which means *healing, safety, deliverance, protection,* and *soundness*, and includes the ministry of angels.[1]

As an heir of salvation, you have a right to benefit from everything salvation has to offer. The Bible says:

Therefore we ought to give the more earnest heed to the things which we have heard [from God's Word], lest at any time we should let them slip. For if the word spoken by angels was stedfast, and every transgression and disobedience received a just recompence of reward; how shall we escape, if we neglect so great salvation . . . ?

HEBREWS 2:1–3

How shall we escape trouble and walk in the confidence of God if we neglect our salvation? How can we escape all the adverse circumstances we're faced with if we neglect the great healing, deliverance, safety, soundness, protection, and ministry of angels? How can we escape trouble if we don't take advantage of what was made available to us when we became born again?

We simply cannot escape trouble if we neglect our salvation. However, if we don't neglect our salvation, then salvation becomes our way of escape. Our healing, safety, deliverance, protection, soundness, and the ministry of angels become our way of escape.

Pay Attention!

All the things included in *soteria* are available to us, but in order to attain them, we have to be willing to pay for them.

What do we have to pay? What is the medium of exchange? *Attention.* The Bible says:

> . . . *attend to my words; incline thine ear unto my sayings.*
>
> *Let thine eyes look right on, and let thine eyelids look straight before thee.*
>
> *Turn not to the right hand nor to the left. . . .*
>
> PROVERBS 4:20,25,27

All we have to do to receive the benefits of our salvation is to give heed, or pay attention to, the things that we have heard from the Word of God. We must be careful not to neglect those benefits or let them slip out of our consciousness.

The Good News that will remain is that Jesus paid the price for this great salvation for each of us. We don't have to buy it, because Jesus has already bought it with His blood. With His blood He purchased our healing, soundness, deliverance, protection, and safety.

Don't Give Up

Even though we have been given this great salvation, we can't deny that problems come. In fact, Jesus Himself said in John 16:33, "In the world ye shall have tribulation," so we know that trouble will still come.

However, when Jesus spoke of "the world," He was referring to the world system—its values and its way of doing things. Don't be surprised when trouble shows up, because according to Jesus, as long as you are in the world—and particularly as long as you are operating according to the world system—trouble will come. However, Jesus also said, "These things I have spoken unto you, that in me ye might have peace."

Peace comes from hearing the words that Jesus has spoken. Jesus said, "In the world ye shall have tribulation: but be of good cheer; I have overcome the world" (John 16:33). Peace comes from the Word of God, from the *Word system*, from God's way of doing things. In the world system we will have tribulation, but in the Word system we will have peace.

Therefore, we have to choose in which system to operate while we live in this world. As born-again believers, we are *in* this world, but we are not *of* this world. We live physically in this natural world, but we don't operate according to the system of this world. Operating in the system of God's Word produces peace.

The time we finally understand this is when the Devil will seek to steal that peace. Every chance he gets, he will throw up a big mountain of problems in our path to distract us so that he can steal the Word of God from us, preventing the Word from impacting our lives. We must remember, though, that the ultimate victory has already been won. Jesus has overcome the world. (John 16:33.) Therefore, when problems arise in this world, we don't have to give up, cave in, or quit. We can walk in the confidence of God over the problems.

God is in control, and if we will do what the Bible tells us to do in between the prayer of faith and the answer, trouble will not be able to overcome us. We will be able to walk in the confidence of God despite any problem that may arise.

Overcome Weariness

To continue walking in the confidence of God, we have to overcome one of the biggest enemies of faith: weariness. Often, the answers to our prayers seem so far away that we become tired of believing the promises God has given to us in His Word. When we get weary, we can be tempted to give up and quit. Hebrews 12:3 warns us of the dangers of weariness: "For consider him that endured such contradiction of sinners against himself, lest ye be wearied *and faint in your minds*."

If we allow ourselves to become weary, we will faint in our minds. The word *faint* means "to give up, cave in and quit."[2] The mind is the arena for battles of faith. We win or lose each battle because of what happens in our minds.

The Bible tells us to consider Jesus—to keep the eyes of our faith fixed on Jesus and His Word. If we do not, we will become weary and be tempted to faint: to give up, cave in, and quit right in the middle of the fight of faith.

Forty Days and Nights on Two Meals

Even Elijah, one of the greatest prophets of the Old Testament, became weary. Under the anointing of God, Elijah called down fire and rain, defeated 400 prophets of Baal and had them killed, and outran chariot horses. (1 Kings 18:46.)

However, when he found out that Queen Jezebel planned to kill him to avenge her prophets, Elijah got up and ran for his life. He was so scared that he ran a day's journey out into the wilderness, sat down under a juniper tree, and prayed that he might die. (1 Kings 19:1–4.) Two days after he had seen God do mighty miracles through him, Elijah was so depressed and weary that he was ready to give up and die.

Do you know what caused Elijah to lose his confidence in God? He forgot to refill himself with the words of God until he overflowed. He neglected his heavenly supply and didn't replace what he had poured out while doing the miracles. He allowed himself to become weary, and his weariness made space in his heart to occupy. Consequently, the Devil was able to come in and put fear in Elijah's heart.

God had to send an angel two days in a row to cook Elijah a meal, and Elijah had to eat and drink of this heavenly food before he had the strength to go on again. However, when he partook of the nourishment the Lord sent him, he was able to travel 40 days and 40 nights on the strength of just those two meals! (v. 8.)

We must take a lesson from Elijah's experience and remember to keep ourselves nourished with the Word. Otherwise, we too may become weary and faint in our minds (give up, cave in, and quit) when we're waiting for the answers to our prayers. Therefore, no matter how many problems the Devil throws our way, we must keep our eyes on Jesus and His Word.

Getting to the Other Side

A good reason to keep our eyes on God and His Word in the midst of problems is that it helps us to remember that God Himself never gets weary. He never faints or gives up. He is in control over the entire universe. He has promised that no matter how long we have to wait for the manifestation of His promise, as long as we serve Him while we wait, our waiting will never be in vain.

> *Hast thou not known? hast thou not heard, that the everlasting God, the Lord, the Creator of the ends of the earth, fainteth not, neither is weary? there is no searching of his understanding.*

> ISAIAH 40:28

Isn't it good to know that we have a God in heaven who will not give up, cave in, or quit? He is the best Person with whom to make a covenant. Humans are capable of quitting, caving in, and giving up, but we have a God in heaven who never faints or gets weary.

We can't weary God. Sometimes we might think, *God has to be fed up with me by now. He must be tired of listening to me. He probably doesn't even want anything to do with me anymore!* However, our being troubled in difficult times will never weary God. His mercy endures forever. In other words, His mercy outlasts any trouble.

God can outlast anything just for the joy of seeing one person come into His arms, saying, "Lord, I'm Yours. Everything I have, everything I am. I'm Yours."

Renewed Strength

I am so glad that God never gets weary or faints; however, His mercy does not stop there. He also renews the strength of those who are feeling weary and about to faint.

> *He giveth power to the faint; and to them that have no might he increaseth strength. Even the youths shall faint and be weary, and the young men shall utterly fall: but they that wait upon the Lord shall renew their strength; they shall mount up with wings as eagles; they shall run, and not be weary; and they shall walk, and not faint.*

> Isaiah 40:29–31

Through the prophet Isaiah, God has promised that as we wait on Him, He will give us strength to get through any problem. As we spend time with Him, He not only renews our physical strength, but He also renews our inner strength to the point where we can "mount up with wings as eagles."

In order to understand the significance of this promise, we need to understand some things about eagles' wings.

First, it's important to note that the wings of an eagle are specifically designed to enable the bird to cruise at high altitudes. At 80,000 feet, eagles cruise about twice as high as jet aircraft normally fly.

Second, the eagle's wings are designed to lock down in position to gain altitude so that if the eagle is caught in a storm, it can rise above it. No amount of turbulence can overcome the locked down position of an eagle's wings. The eagle with locked down wing rises higher and higher until it is eventually out of the storm and flying above the turbulence. Instead of being subject to the storm, the eagle soars above it.

Likewise, according to God's promise in Isaiah 40:31, we can put on eagle's wings by waiting on the Lord and focusing on His promises. Then, in times of trouble, our eagle's wings will lock down and take us to higher altitudes. When life gets a little rough, we will rise above the problems.

No matter how high the storm or how thick the clouds, God has equipped you with eagle's wings so that you can come up, out, and rise above your circumstances. You shall mount up with wings as eagles; you shall run and not be weary; you shall walk and not faint—all because of what you do in the middle of the problems.

When you set your mind on the promises of God, you are mounting up with wings as an eagle. When you put guards over your ears and eyes to keep out the lies Satan brings to oppose God's promises, your strength is being renewed. If problems show up, you have the ability to rise above the storm. Below there may be hail falling, wind blowing, and lightning flashing, but you will soar above it all, saying, "There's nothing but sunshine up here."

When we wait on the Lord, we will not get weary and faint. When we spend time with the Lord to the point that His Word is overflowing from our hearts, we will naturally walk in the confidence of God. This requires that we not allow afflictions and persecutions, the cares of this world, the deceitfulness of riches, or desires for anything in the world's system to distract us from spending time with God.

God Is in Control

When problems come, don't you want to be with the One who has everything under control? Even when you don't think God is in control, He is. Even when it looks as if everything is going to pieces around you, God is in control.

Do you remember the story about the widow in 1 Kings 17? In the middle of a drought, she said, "I'm going to use up the last of my flour and oil to make some bread for me and my boy. Then we're going to die."

However, her trouble and fear did not stop God. He stretched her resources: "For the jar of flour was not used up and the jug of oil did not run dry, in keeping with the word of the Lord . . ." (v. 16 NIV). No human being was putting flour into the jar or oil into the jug. God was stretching the woman's resources.

If you are in the middle of financial difficulty, you can rest on this promise: "God shall supply all your need according to his riches in glory by Christ Jesus" (Phil. 4:19). God can stretch your resources, because He is in control. If all you have is $2.50 and some coupons, you will be amazed at how much it can do if you put it in God's hands. God is in control. In order to maintain your peace and walk in the confidence of God, you must believe that. When you can't figure out why circumstances are the way they are, you have to be able to say from your spirit, "That's all right. God is in control. I don't understand how this will end, but I won't fear because God is in control. I'm not afraid of what people can do to me, be-cause God is in control. I won't receive the bad report, be-cause God is in control. And if God is in control, it will be all right."

If you can say that from your heart, then it will be all right. The reason it will be all right is that you will not be in control. You will have turned the control over to God. When the

Almighty is responsible for getting you to your proper destination, you will get there—as long as you keep yourself set.

Just as a pilot has to properly set his or her instruments to guide a plane toward its desired destination, so must you properly set your spirit to head toward the promises God has given you. You do that by setting your attention and affection on God and His Word.

In an airplane, the pilot can't figure out the way just by looking out the window: Up in the air, everything looks the same. Therefore, the pilot has to rely on the instruments being properly set.

Likewise, we cannot decide where to go just based on what we see happening around us. Circumstances can't guide us, because they are always subject to change. Instead, we must set our course by relying on the Word of God. We must set our headings to take us where we want to go. Then we can turn control over to God, the autopilot, and sit back and monitor the instruments.

When we reach the promise, we get to possess the land because it is ours. It is what God has provided for us. We will reach that land of promise when we walk in the confidence of God, acknowledging that He is in control.

You are going to be all right. From this point on, you do not have to be troubled. Problems may show up, but you do not have to let them affect you. The devil may claim to be in control of your circumstances, but when you walk in the confidence of God, you can just laugh in his face and say, "Get out of here, devil. You're not in control. God is in control. Nobody but Jesus sits on the throne of my life; therefore, I will have righteousness. I will have peace. I will have joy in the Holy Ghost. I bind principalities and powers and wicked spirits in heavenly places, and God is perfecting that which concerns me, in Jesus' name. Amen."

You will be amazed at how small the problems become when you realize that God is in control of everything that concerns you. Get ready to walk in the confidence of God every day. Prepare to soar with eagle's wings and with the renewed strength that you will find when you wait on the Lord, because He is in control.

Study Questions

1. What types of troubles are you facing in your life right now?

_____

_____

_____

_____

_____

2. How do you normally respond when trouble comes or pressures start to build?

_____

_____

_____

_____

_____

3. Why does weariness make us susceptible to losing our confidence?

_____

_____

_____

_____

_____

4. In what ways can we renew our strength?

_____

_____

_____

_____

_____

5. How would you describe your walk with Christ?

_____

_____

_____

_____

_____

**Take a few minutes to write out a list of
the issues you're facing, and what
you'd like to see happen in your life.**

_____

_____

_____

_____

_____

Doing Our Part

GOD'S BEING IN control doesn't mean that we have no part in the process of walking in the confidence of God. Overcoming problems is not just God's responsibility. We also have a responsibility and a part to play. There are things we have to do in order for the system that God has put in place to operate in our lives.

In order to walk in the confidence of God, we need to discover our responsibility in the process of maintaining our confidence even in troubled times. Remember that Jesus said:

> These things I have spoken unto you, that in me ye might have peace. In the world ye shall have tribulation: but be of good cheer; I have overcome the world.
>
> JOHN 16:33

We cannot deny that problems have invaded this planet. Without a doubt, trouble is everywhere. Every day, we can turn on the news and see terrible end-of-the-age events that Jesus described in Matthew 24. However, in John 16:33, Jesus gives us a significant message: "I've spoken to you so that in Me you might have peace." As we have noted, Jesus' words—the Word of God—bring peace.

We have scratched the surface of the significance of these Scriptures, but now let's go a little deeper to discover how to walk in the confidence of God in troubled times.

A Covenant of Peace

The book of Isaiah says that God has established a covenant of peace with us:

> *For the mountains shall depart, and the hills be removed; but my kindness shall not depart from thee, neither shall the covenant of my peace be removed, saith the Lord that hath mercy on thee.*

> ISAIAH 54:10

By establishing this covenant of peace, God has done His part in the process of our walking in His confidence. He has made the covenant and ratified it in His Son's blood, which enables us to do our part, so that this covenant can be effective in our lives.

Satan's part in this process is to keep us from inheriting this covenant. His attacks are an attempt to disable us from walking in the confidence of God. To overcome the Devil's attempts to hold us back from our covenant of peace, we must learn to do our part.

I heard a story one time that reinforces the fact that we do have a part in deciding the condition of our lives. The story went something like this: A man saw the Devil sitting on a wall outside a church, crying. The man said, "What's the matter, Satan? Why are you crying?" The Devil said, "I'm tired of these Christians lying about me. I'm tired of them blaming me for all their problems. I'm getting blamed for stuff I didn't even do!"

The point is that you and I must take responsibility for what is and what is not happening in our lives. Galatians 6:7 says, "Whatsoever a man soweth, that shall he also reap." In other words, our condition in life is based on the seeds that we have sown in the past. If we don't like the condition of our lives, we have to change it by changing the seeds we sow.

The Word Brings Peace

In order to reap peace in our lives, we need to sow a specific seed in our hearts. In John 16:33, Jesus identified that seed: "In me ye might have peace." We know that Jesus and the Word are one because John 1:1 and 14 say, "In the beginning was the Word, and the Word was with God, and the Word was God. . . . And the Word was made flesh, (and we beheld his glory, the glory as of the only begotten of the Father,) full of grace and truth." Therefore, in context, we can see that we will have peace in the Word: "In me [Jesus, the Word of God] ye might have peace."

If you want peace in your life, you need to sow the Word into your heart. God is interested in your inheriting the covenant of peace. You just have to be watchful because there are certain tricks that the devil will try to use to remove the seed of the Word from your heart. (Matt. 14:19–23.) Most of us have lost seed to the devil in one or more areas of our lives. However, we must learn how to keep the Word alive and flourishing in our hearts so that we can receive the harvest of peace and everything that God desires to give us.

Seek the Things Above

Colossians 3:1 says:

> If ye then be risen with Christ [the Anointed One and His Anointing], seek those things which are above, where Christ [the Anointed One and His Anointing] sitteth on the right hand of God.

Paul is not talking about seeking something that is right over our heads. He is talking about seeking something that is higher. *The Amplified Bible* says to seek "the higher things" (v. 2). We are to seek something that is on a higher level.

The "things which are above" are found in the Word of God. The Word of God is higher than the world system. We will not be able to reach the things that are above if we do not get in the Word. If we want to attain the higher things, we cannot read our Bible only on Sundays. We cannot act like Christians only at church. The Devil works every day to steal the Word from us; therefore, if we want to live in the covenant of peace and walk in the confidence of God, we have to make a decision to get into the Word of God every day.

Paul goes on:

> *Set your affection on things above, not on things on the earth. For ye are dead, and your life is hid with Christ in God.*
>
> COLOSSIANS 3:2,3

The Amplified Bible says:

> *If then you have been raised with Christ [to a new life, thus sharing His resurrection from the dead], aim at and seek the [rich, eternal treasures] that are above,*

where Christ is, seated at the right hand of God. And set your minds and keep them set on what is above (the higher things), not on the things that are on the earth. For [as far as this world is concerned] you have died, and your [new, real] life is hidden with Christ in God.

COLOSSIANS 3:1–3

In this passage, we see very clearly that we have a part to play in walking in the confidence of God. We must set our minds on higher things. This is our responsibility, not God's. We cannot say, "Heavenly Father, I pray in the name of Jesus that You keep my mind set on Your Word." God will not do that for us. Setting our minds on the Word is our responsibility. Until we take some responsibility for our lives as Christians, we will not reach the promises that God has waiting for us. There are certain things God will not do because He has placed the responsibility in our hands.

One of those things is filling us with the Word. He won't pick up the Book and read it to us while we sleep. We have to read the Bible for ourselves.

Some things that happen in our lives are neither God's fault nor the Devil's fault. They are our fault. It is our fault some of our troubles have come, because we failed to take responsibility for our actions. We have failed to do our part so God could do His part to make the system operate as it should.

Not on Earthly Things

Colossians 3:2 warns us not to set our minds on the things of the earth. For example, God doesn't want us to watch the news 24 hours a day. God wants us to keep our minds clear from the things of earth, and He has a reason for this. If we set our minds on this world, our hearts will be flooded with this world's cares.

Satan wants us to hear the words that promote the cares of this world. He wants to infiltrate us with those cares, concerns, and worries. He wants us to hear his words because they produce fear; he wants us to be distracted from the Word of God because it produces faith.

Let Not Your Heart Be Troubled

Jesus gave us these faith-producing words in John 14:27:

> *Peace I leave with you, my peace I give unto you: not as the world giveth, give I unto you. Let not your heart be troubled, neither let it be afraid.*

In this verse, Jesus is telling us that we are responsible for the condition of our hearts. In order to walk in the confidence of God, we need to remember three applications from this verse.

First, we are responsible for what goes into us. The Devil may try to put something in us, but we are still responsible for what gets into our hearts through our ears and eyes. Second, we are responsible for making sure our hearts are not troubled. Third, we are responsible for making sure our hearts are not filled with fear.

We cannot allow our hearts to be full of fear. Where there is no fear, there can be no trouble. Problems may be all around us, but if we aren't filled with fear we won't be troubled by them. Our hearts will not be troubled if they are not afraid.

Fear and Faith Oppose One Another

Fear and faith stand in opposition to one another. Romans 10:17 tells us, "Faith cometh by hearing, and hearing by the word of God." Conversely, fear comes by hearing the words of the Devil.

The Devil wants you to hear his words. Because he is the god of the world system, he wants you to hear the words that come from the world system. He wants you to fill your heart with his words so you will operate in fear, which is contaminated faith.

Pay close attention to what I am saying: To walk in fear is to walk in faith. If you fear cancer, then what you are actually doing is having faith and confidence in cancer's ability to kill you. If you fear losing your job, you are actually putting faith and confidence in the fact that you will lose you job. If you fear being mugged when you go to the ATM at night, you have faith and confidence in the ability of a mugger to attack and rob you. When you operate in fear, you are operating in the faith and confidence that the thing you fear has the ability to destroy you.

To walk in the confidence of God, you have to reverse the process. Instead of having fear, which is faith that the Devil can do a certain thing in your life, you must have faith that the Word of God can do what it says it can do in your life.

Your faith is a force that will produce whatever is in your heart. As a result, whatever is in your heart will motivate you to give room for either God or the devil to bring that thing to pass.

I know it sounds strange, but fear is the faith of the devil. Fear is what the devil needs to bring certain things to pass in your life.

Is fear in your life? If so, you must move it out with the overflow of the Word of God. If you do not, a door stands open for Satan to say, "I have the right to bring to pass the thing that you fear." When fear is in your heart, it outweighs the Word of God. That means in your heart fear takes precedence over the Word of God because you are more filled with fear than with the Word of God.

The Importance of Guarding Our Hearts

Our decision as to whether or not we will guard our hearts is what determines whether we will be troubled or walking in the confidence of God. Can you recall times when you wish you hadn't heard certain things? Your day was going fine until somebody told you something you wished he'd kept to himself. That bad report occupied your thinking. Even though you might have just gotten out of Bible study, those unpleasant words invaded your heart.

Through those negative words, the Devil was trying to affect your life in a particular way. Jesus talks about this in Mark 4:

> *The sower soweth the word. And these are they by the way side, where the word is sown; but when they have heard, Satan cometh immediately, and taketh away the word that was sown in their hearts. And these are they likewise which are sown on stony ground; who, when they have heard the word, immediately receive it with gladness; and have no root in themselves, and so endure but for a time: afterward, when affliction or persecution ariseth for the word's sake, immediately they are offended. And these are they which are sown among thorns; such as hear the word, and the cares of this world, and the deceitfulness of riches, and the lusts of other things entering in, choke the word, and it becometh unfruitful.*

> MARK 4:14–19

Verse 19 says that the cares of this world have the ability to choke the Word—to make it unfruitful. Satan wants to fill our hearts with the cares of this world. He wants to use the cares in our lives—our marriages, families, jobs, economy, nation, and world—to fill us with care. If he is successful at persuading us to focus on those cares, even though we may be going to church and reading the Bible, those cares will choke what little bit of Word we receive.

We have to fill ourselves with the Word every day. The Word we receive at church on Sundays is not enough to fill us to overflowing so that the cares of the world cannot penetrate our hearts. Some believers are defeated, not because they aren't getting the Word, but because they are getting more care than Word. Therefore, they never see their harvest. The cares of this world are in them so abundantly that they choke up what Word they do receive. There must be enough Word in us to overcome the cares that are tossed at us every day.

Until the Word becomes our life, it will never become our reality. The cares of this world will enter in and choke the Word so it cannot bring forth the fruit it was designed to bring forth. If we are so busy dealing with the cares of our world, the cares will occupy our attention and distract us from the Word. The cares will grow like weeds and overcome our hearts if they are left unchecked by the power of the Word of God.

Negative Meditation

Most of us have spent all of our lives carrying around the cares of the world. We have pretended to know how to handle them, when actually we have only been able to watch them grow. In fact, by carrying our cares around we've placed ourselves in a position where the Word of God has become unfruitful in our lives.

If we allow them to, the cares of the world will choke the Word out of our hearts until we spend all our time feeding on the cares of the world. When we do this, our minds become occupied with fear. We worry about things that haven't even happened yet.

Just as fear and faith oppose one another, so do worry and meditation. Joshua 1:8 says that if we meditate on the Word day and night, we will make our way prosperous and have success. Conversely, if we meditate on the words of the Devil day and night, we will make ourselves "prosperous" and "successful" in the things of the Devil.

For instance, if you worry that your son will become a drug addict, you will prosper and have good success in that negative meditation. As a result, you may soon have a cocaine addict in your household. If allowed, worry and fear—the "faith" of the Devil—will direct the forces in your heart in the wrong way, and those forces will produce results in your life.

Don't Wait

You may be thinking, *I assumed it was just natural to worry. I don't think it's possible not to.*

At the moment, your circumstances may seem absolutely crushing. It may seem impossible to do anything but worry, but why is that? Could it be that up till now you have spent more time focusing on the cares of this world than on the promises of God?

We cannot wait until we are bombarded with problems to begin cramming the Word into our hearts. For example, we can't wait until the doctor gives us a negative report to study healing Scriptures. Filling our hearts with the Word must be a lifestyle so we can live it day by day.

What God Understands

Most of us walk around with our hearts filled more with the cares of the world than with the Word of God. The limited time we spend in God's Word is causing us to miss out on some valuable things. As long as we don't think we *really* have to do all that it takes to fill our hearts to the point of overflow, we will not walk in the confidence of God and reach the highest potential to which He has called us.

So often, we use our famous excuse: "God understands." Oh, yes, He understands. What He understands is that we are not going to receive what we are believing Him for, because we have not done our part to make it happen.

For example, someone might say, "God understands why I didn't tithe." Yes, He understands, but He understands that the heavens are closed to this person and the devourer will not be rebuked for his sake. He understands why his car keeps breaking down and his property keeps being damaged: He has not given Him the tithe that will enable God to rebuke the Devil and say, "Stop! No more! You can't touch that."

If you are tithing and obeying the Word, then regardless of what happens, God has already made a way out. He has designed this covenant of peace, and He has done His part. Now you have to do your part. You have to spend more time meditating on the Word than you do worrying about the cares of the world.

Did You Know?

Somebody came up to me one time and said, "Did you know Michael Jackson got married?" I looked at him as if to say, "Did he write me to let me know?" No, I didn't know. I didn't care. I spend my time reading, listening to and speaking the Word of God, and getting built up in the Holy Spirit. I don't care whether some entertainer got married. That is none of my business. Knowing that information will not help me.

The Word of God contains all of the information you and I need to know. My question is not, "Did you know this happened to this person?" My question is, "Did you know that by Jesus' stripes we are healed?" "Did you know that God says He knows how to deliver us out of all our trouble?" "Did you know that we have a secret place of the Most High?" "Did you know that there is power in the name of Jesus?" "Did you know that the anointing will give us victory?"

Believers, let's get into the Good News and lay the cares of this world to rest! Let's not spend our time watching soap operas. If we do, when problems arise, we will have melodrama in our hearts. That won't help us get out of the problems. It will keep us in them.

Instead of spending our time filling our hearts with the cares of the world, let's spend our time filling our hearts with the Word of God. Imagine the difference we could make in this world if we would replace the time we spend staying current on worldly events with time spent reading and confessing the Word, writing it on our hearts.

Some people think, *It doesn't take all that. God understands I have a career and I don't have time for the Word.* No, God does not "understand" that. He understands that they have made their careers a god instead of Him. He understands that they are not filling themselves with the Word of God but with the cares of this world.

The Only Place for Care

According to the Bible, there is only one thing we are anointed to do with care, and that is to cast it on God.

Humble yourselves therefore under the mighty hand of God, that he may exalt you in due time: casting all your care upon him; for he careth for you.

1 PETER 5:6,7

In order to cast our cares on the Lord, we must first humble ourselves. Simply stated, humility is submission, compliance and the submission of oneself to the commandments of God. Conversely, pride is rebellion against and disobedience toward God's commands.

When we submit ourselves to God, we are submitting ourselves to His Word. We are considering the Word before we consider the cares of this world.

Submitting oneself to the Word brings the anointing and power that the Word contains. Peter says that we are to humble ourselves "under the mighty hand of God." Remember, when Elijah got under the hand of God, he outran horses and chariots. (1 Kings 18:46.) Peter is saying that when we get under the mighty hand of God, we can expect the anointing to come into our lives.

God wants to exalt us. In order for that to happen, though, we must submit so that "He may exalt [us] in due time." "Due season" always comes. We will be exalted when we position ourselves to be exalted. That position is in humility under the commandments of God.

If we step out from under the hand of God and say, "I'm going to do what I want to do," we will position ourselves to fall. However, when we let God bring us up, He becomes the One responsible for maintaining us in that higher position. This is what 1 Peter 5:6 is telling us: "Humble yourselves . . . that he may exalt you. . . ."

Cast All Your Care

Once we have learned to humble ourselves, we can take the next step and walk in the confidence of God:

Casting all your care upon him; for he careth for you.

1 PETER 5:7

Notice that we are to give up all of our cares. We are to cast our family cares, our job cares, our financial cares, our physical cares, our spiritual cares—*all* of our cares on God.

Who do we think we are, walking around maintaining the cares of life as if we were anointed to do something about them? We have never been anointed to do something about our cares except to cast them on God! We are called and anointed to cast them on the Lord!

When a fisherman *casts* his line out, it goes far from him to another place. That is what we are supposed to do with our cares. We are to cast them far from us to another place—right into God's hands. Then we are to let go of them. God wants to get rid of them, and He can't do that until we do.

You are not supposed to be walking around full of care. God is saying to you, "Cast your cares on Me. I'm equipped to handle your cares. I know what to do with them. I know how to destroy them. If you'll just let Me, I will demonstrate that I know what I'm doing."

Actually, it is an act of rebellion to maintain cares, trying to figure out what to do and how to fix a problem alone. So many of us have said, "Oh, dear Lord, how am I going to do this?" We need to stop ourselves right there. We are not supposed to know how to do it. We are supposed to get rid of it. That care is not our problem. It is not our responsibility. We grieve the Spirit of God when we hold on to our cares, because we stop Him from doing what He desires to do with them.

Don't walk around in false humility, saying, "I'll be all right after a while." You can be all right now by faith, if you will cast away those cares.

On the Lord

The Bible says to cast your cares on the Lord. It does not say to cast them on the pastor of your church. Sometimes Christians think they should dump everything on the pastor, the deacons, or the counselors.

As a pastor, I have had to learn to get up in the morning and say, "Good morning, Jesus. I don't care." Then when people try to dump their problems on me, I can avoid taking on their cares—cares that do not belong to me.

You and I are not supposed to carry our own cares, much less anyone else's. The Bible does not tell us to bring all our cares to the pastor or to each other. It says to cast our cares on God because He cares for us.

God cares for you much more than any human being could ever think about caring for you, so do not hold on to your cares or give them to someone else. Give them to God, because He is the only One who knows what to do with them. Your job is to get in the Word, be in Christ, and cast your cares on the Lord. Allow Him to care for you, and start walking in His confidence. When God is taking care of your cares, you can be sure that He is leading you to success, even in troubled times.

Study Questions

1. How would you describe a life that has God in control?

_____

_____

_____

_____

_____

2. If a friend told you she needed peace, what would you say to her?

_____

_____

_____

_____

3. How can a Christian keep his or her mind on "the higher things"?

_____

_____

_____

_____

4. In what ways do fear and faith oppose one another in your life?

_____

_____

_____

_____

5. How can you cast your cares onto the Lord?

_____

_____

_____

_____

Take a few minutes to write a prayer to the Lord, casting your cares onto Him and asking Him to fill your mind with the higher things.

_____

_____

_____

_____

3

The Key to Success

Even though problems may be all around us, we don't have to be troubled. However, problems will not disappear off the face of the earth just because we learn to use the weapons we have available to overcome them. Our objective is to use those weapons so that we can walk in the confidence of God in the face of problems.

If we want to walk in the confidence of God during troubled times, we must do our part. Our level of success will be determined by our confidence level in God and in His Word. Ultimately, the degree of confidence we have in God's Word will determine the degree of our success in this life.

No Word, No Confidence

Having absolute confidence in God and in His Word is the key to success in overcoming trouble in every area of life. The book of Hebrews makes this clear.

The Key to Success

Cast not away therefore your confidence, which hath great recompence of reward.

The writer of Hebrews tells us not to cast our confidence away, not to get rid of it. How does a man cast away his confidence? By casting away the Word of God. If you don't have the Word of God on a certain subject, you won't have confidence in that particular subject.

For instance, if you don't have the Word of God on the subject of sowing and reaping, you won't have confidence in sowing; therefore, you won't experience reaping. If you don't have the Word of God on divine health, you won't experience that either.

Romans 10:17 says, "Faith cometh by hearing, and hearing by the Word of God." It is of such great importance that we hear the Word of God. Doing so gives us confidence in the Word. If we do not have any Word, we definitely will not have confidence in the Word.

The Amplified Bible puts it like this:

Do not, therefore, fling away your fearless confidence, for it carries a great and glorious compensation of reward.

If you hold fast to your confidence, if you hold on tightly to the Word of God, you can expect to be compensated. You will be rewarded for holding on to your confidence in the Word. Your confidence in the Word is your guarantee of compensation. It pays to keep the Word in your life.

The Reward of Diligence

Let me show you a man who held on to his confidence in the Word and was compensated for it. This man is described in Psalm 112:

> *Praise ye the Lord. Blessed is the man that feareth the Lord, that delighteth greatly in his commandments.*

> PSALM 112:1

The word *bless* in this verse means "empowered to prosper."[1] To *prosper* means to be in control of your circumstances.

Psalm 112:1 specifically talks about a man who is empowered through his delight in the Word of God. The fact that he is empowered simply means that he has been given ability. Power and ability have been given to him. He has been empowered to be in control of the outcome.

How is it that a man can be empowered by just delighting in the commandments of God? The Bible says, "Delight thyself also in the Lord: and he shall give thee the desires of thine heart" (Ps. 37:4). Something good always happens to a person who delights in the Word of God.

This man in Psalm 112 is empowered. As a result of his delight in God's Word, verse 2 says "his seed shall be mighty upon the earth: the generation of the upright shall be blessed." Verse 3 continues: "Wealth and riches shall be in his house: and his righteousness endureth for ever."

Jesus' words verify this promise:

> *Seek ye first the kingdom of God, and his righteousness; and all these things shall be added unto you.*
>
> Matthew 6:33

In our quest to obtain the things we need, we have been doing everything except the right thing. What we must do is to seek first the kingdom of God. Instead of trying to figure out how to get all of our physical needs met, we need to delight ourselves in the Word of God because the Word is responsible for putting those physical things in our lives.

Light in the Darkness

The psalmist continues:

> *Unto the upright there ariseth light in the darkness.*
>
> Psalm 112:4

"The upright" is the same man who delights in the commandments of God. The man who delights in God's Word will have light in the darkness. Have you ever had an idea, and you just thought you were the smartest person in the whole world because of it? You just patted yourself on the back and walked around saying, "I'm good! I'm good!"

In truth, the reason you got that great idea is that you were spending time in God's Word. The Bible says that the man who delights in the commandments of God—the man who studies, meditates on, and confesses the Word on a daily basis—doesn't fear darkness because he will always have light arising right in the middle of it.

When you spend time in God's Word and delight yourself in the commandments of God, the revelation—understanding light—of God will explode on the inside of you. I guarantee you there will not be a time when you will not know what to do. However, even if you don't understand it in the natural, God will give you light in the midst of darkness, just because you have delighted yourself in His Word.

I have come up with solutions to problems about which I had no understanding. I have received enlightenment about things for which I had no natural education. However, the light came because of the time I had spent in the Word before the situations arose.

Maybe you have experienced something like this: You are riding in the car, trying to figure something out, and the answer just pops up. It does not come to you because you are smart. It arises from within you because you have been spending time in the Word of God and that Word has gotten inside of you. As a result, just as God has promised, light rises. The idea, the answer to the problem, is compensation for time spent in the Word.

God is faithful. He will always compensate you for time spent in the Word. You are not spending time in the Word for free! God says, "I will compensate you—if you don't cast away your confidence in My Word." In other words, He says, "I'll cash this compensation check if you don't throw it away."

It is wonderful to know that in the middle of darkness, light will rise for the upright person who has been delighting in God's Word. If you have not yet had times of darkness when you didn't know what to do, just wait. They will come. Just delight in the Word of God now so that when the time of darkness comes, you will receive the compensation of light.

Free from Fear

Just because darkness comes, that does not mean you have to be afraid. Psalm 112:5–8 says:

> *A good man sheweth favour, and lendeth: he will guide his affairs with discretion. Surely he shall not be moved for ever: the righteous shall be in everlasting remembrance.*

He shall not be afraid of evil tidings: his heart is fixed, trusting in the Lord. His heart is established, he shall not be afraid, until he see his desire upon his enemies.

The one who delights in the Word of God is not afraid. The reason he is not afraid is that his heart is fixed. What do you think it is fixed on? His heart is fixed on the Lord and His Word. Because he has a fixed heart, he is also free from fear.

Are you walking in the confidence of God, or do you have fear in your heart? If you have fear in your heart, I can tell you why. It is because you don't have the Word in your heart. It's simple, but it's true. If you don't have the Word in your heart, then the Devil will immediately try to occupy that void. However, when your heart is fixed on the Word, you are able to trust in the Lord; as a result, you will not fear.

That is what Jesus is talking about when He says, "Let not your heart be troubled, neither let it be afraid." (John 14:27). We must accept the responsibility given to us through that Scripture. It is our responsibility to not be afraid and to not let our hearts be troubled. The way we do that is to fix our hearts on the Word of God.

Practical Application

I don't want to just tell you, "Get your heart fixed on the Word of God." I want to show you how to do that. People don't do cartwheels when you tell them, "Meditate in the Word of God and that will solve your problem. Spend eight hours a day for five days in the Word of God and you will be healed." This generation wants everything right now!

We need hearts that are established on the Word of God; however, how do we get them to be that way? We do it by speaking Scriptures out loud every day. Personally, I try to say these Scriptures two to three times a day out loud.

In my life, I have identified some of these Scriptures as preventive medicine. What happens is this: I recognize that there are certain things in life that I don't want to go through. Somebody might say, "What if you had to go through this? What would you do?" I don't know what I would do, so I don't want to go through it. For example, I don't want a doctor telling me I have some kind of deadly disease. Therefore, I believe in the preventive method. I believe in preventing those things with Scriptures about healing.

Similarly, I don't want to think about what I'd do if I went broke. I don't want to go through that, so I like the preventive way. I identify Scriptures about God's provision and speak them over my life.

If I didn't know the biblical answers to those nagging questions, then I could easily become afraid; I could become troubled; I could get worried. I could pretend to be a man of faith, but actually be afraid on the inside. Thankfully, though, I learned something in a troubled time in my life. When I was feeling as if I was about to crumble, give up, and cave in, the Lord spoke to my heart: *Practice what you preach.* I did it, and it has been working for me all this time.

The Answer to All Problems

I absolutely believe with all my heart that the answer to all of our problems is to make sure our hearts are fixed on the Word on a daily basis. The Bible says, "Set your minds and keep them set" (Col. 3:2 AMP). This requires consistency.

I believe this works in my life! I believe that when I set my mind and keep my mind set, I am keeping myself set toward a successful and victorious outcome. I refuse to let a day go by without fixing my heart. Therefore, each day I have a peaceful, worry-free day. I have no anxiety. It doesn't matter what happens during that day, because I can rely on what I have done in my heart every day.

Somebody might say, "You know, it doesn't take all that to have a successful day."

Yes, I believe it does. I don't believe that one hour per week in church on Sunday is enough to cause us to live successful, victorious Christian lives. I believe it takes a daily commitment to get our hearts operating in the overflow and ourselves walking in the confidence of God.

Daily Confessions[2]

This is why I fix my heart on the Word daily, and I do this by confessing the Scriptures over my life. These Scriptures address specific areas in my life.

Worry and Fear

For example, this is what I say about worry and fear every day:

"I am the body of Christ and Satan has no power over me, for I overcome evil with good. I am of God and have overcome Satan, for greater is He who is in me than he who is in the world. I will fear no evil, for You are with me. Lord, Your Word and Your Spirit comfort me. I am far from oppression, and fear does not come near me. I won't be depressed today, Lord. No weapon formed against me prospers, for my righteousness is of You. Whatsoever I do prospers, for I am like a tree that is planted by the rivers of water. I am delivered from the evils of this present world, for it is Your will concerning me that I be delivered from evil. No evil befalls me; neither does any plague come near my dwelling, for You have given Your angels charge over me, and they keep me in all my ways. In my pathway is life, and there is no death. I am not dying any time soon, Devil.

"I am a doer of the Word of God, and I am blessed in my deeds. I am happy in those things that I do, because I am a doer of the Word of God. I take the shield of faith, which is the Word of God, and I quench every fiery dart that the wicked one brings against me. Christ has redeemed me from the curse of the law; therefore, I forbid any sickness or disease to come on this body. Every disease, germ, and virus that touches this body dies instantly, in the name of Jesus. Every organ and every tissue of this body functions in the perfection in which You created it to function. I forbid any malfunction in this body, in the name of Jesus. I am an overcomer, and I overcome by the blood of the Lamb and the word of my testimony.

"I am submitted to God, and the Devil flees from me because I resist him in the name of Jesus. The Word of God is forever settled in heaven; therefore, I establish His Word on this earth. Great is the peace of my children, for they are taught of You."

Weight Control

To control my weight, I speak these words over my body:

"I don't desire to eat so much that I become overweight. I present my body to You, Lord; my body is the temple of the Holy Spirit, who dwells in me. I am not my own; I am bought with a price. Therefore, in the name of Jesus, I refuse to overeat. Body, settle down, in the name of Jesus, and conform to the Word of God. I mortify, kill, put to death, the desires of this body and command it to come in line with the Word of God."

Material Needs

These are the words I speak regarding material needs, so that I will never lack anything:

"Christ has redeemed me from the curse of the law. Christ has redeemed me from poverty. Christ has redeemed me from sickness. Christ has redeemed me from spiritual death. For poverty, He has given me wealth. For sickness, He has given me health. For death, He has given me eternal life. It is true according to the Word of God, and I delight myself in You, Lord. As such, You give me the desires of my heart. I have given, and it is given to me. Good measure, pressed down, shaken together, running over, do men give unto my bosom. For with what measure I mete, it is measured to me. I sow bountifully; therefore, I reap bountifully. I give cheerfully, and You have made all grace abound toward me. I, having all sufficiency for all things, abound in all good works. There is no lack, for You have supplied all my needs according to Your riches in glory. You are my shepherd, and I do not want, because Jesus was made poor, that I through His poverty might have abundance. For He came that I might have life and have it more abundantly. I, having received abundance of grace and the gift of righteousness, do reign as king in life by Jesus Christ. You take pleasure in the prosperity of Your servant—that's me! Abraham's blessings are mine."

Wisdom and Guidance

These are the words I speak for wisdom and guidance:

"The Spirit of truth abides in me and teaches me all things, and He guides me into truth. Therefore, I confess I have perfect knowledge of every situation and every circumstance, for I have the wisdom of God. I trust in You, Lord, with all my heart, and I lean not unto my own understanding. In all my ways I acknowledge You, and You direct my path. You perfect that which concerns me. I let the Word of Christ dwell in me richly in all wisdom. I follow the Good Shepherd and I know His voice, and the voice of a stranger I do not follow.

"Jesus is made unto me wisdom, righteousness, sanctification, and redemption; therefore, I confess I have the wisdom of God, and I am the righteousness of God in Christ Jesus. I am filled with the knowledge of the Lord's will in all wisdom and spiritual understanding. I am a new creation in Christ. I am Your workmanship, Lord, created in Christ Jesus; therefore, I have the mind of Christ, and the wisdom of God is formed in me. I have put off the old man and have put on the new man, which was renewed in knowledge after the image of Him who created me. I have received the spirit of wisdom and revelation in the knowledge of Him. The eyes of my understanding are being enlightened. I am not conformed to this world, but I am transformed by the renewing of my mind. My mind is renewed with the Word of God, and I am increasing in the knowledge of God. I am strengthened with all might according to Your glorious power in Jesus' name."

The Results

Every day I speak the Word over my life. I just go on and on speaking these promises for about 20 minutes. When I get up, I fear nothing. My heart is fixed, trusting in the Lord.

Tongue and Heart

Some people get upset with this confession business. They wonder, "Why do you have to say it out loud? Why can't you say it to yourself?" The reason it is important to speak the Word aloud to yourself is that the mouth is involved with the heart. If we want to get our hearts fixed, we need our mouths to do it.

Look at the following Scriptures:

> *. . . my tongue is the pen of a ready writer.*

> PSALM 45:1

> *My son, forget not my law; but let thine heart keep my commandments.*
> *. . . write them upon the table of thine heart.*

> PROVERBS 3:1,3

To write God's commandments on our hearts, we have to use our tongues. If the tongue is the pen and the heart is the table, then we must use our mouths to write the Word on our hearts.

By speaking the Word over my life every particular day, I get my heart fixed on the Word of God. When I pray, I spend some time confessing the Word over every area of my life so I can speak the Word of God to that area and fill my heart with that Word.

The people who think they don't need to do this are the ones who have the same problems every day. The problems are the result of fear, the negative information that comes into their hearts through their eyes or ears. Therefore, we need to set ourselves up differently. When the negative information comes through our eyes or ears, the Word of God should rise up, meet it head-on, and say, "You can't affect this one. Get out of here! I was here first."

As a result of saying the Word out loud, you will have filled your heart with the Word to the point that Satan's words can find no room to occupy. The overflow of the Word will just wash the Devil's words right out.

I Dare You!

Confessing the Word out loud is actually putting Jesus on the throne of your life and putting the Word in your heart. This is something very practical that every believer can do.

I dare you to do this! If you have been struggling with worry, then I challenge you to put the Word inside of you concerning not being anxious. Then when the temptation to worry comes up, the Word meets it head-on and says, "Not today!"

If you have been struggling with fear of lack, then I challenge you to fill yourself to overflowing with the Word of God regarding His provision. Then, when a bill comes, the Word will meet the fear of lack head-on and say, "No, you'll not affect him today!"

If you have been fighting overeating, then I challenge you to fill up your heart with the Word regarding self-control. Then when the temptation to overeat and the spirit of gluttony assault you, the first thing that rises up before you order that next plate will be the Word, saying, "No, you cannot touch him!"

Where Success Begins

When you put the Word in your heart, God will compensate you for the time spent in the Word! Your entire life can change if you will just do this very practical, simple exercise every day. I already know it works, and I want you to experience the victory that God promises all who will set their minds on Him and His Word.

I encourage you to find Scriptures for your own circumstances and your own situation. Don't confine yourself just to the Scriptures on protection, prosperity, and healing. For instance, you might be afraid of being fired, losing your job, or being unable to support your family. In that case, you need to look up all the Scriptures about who God says you are. You need to meditate on the Scriptures about the favor of God. You need to understand that once God opens the door, no man can close the door that God has opened. Soon, you will have yourself so built up in the confidence of God that even if you were the last one your company hired, you can say to the one who was first hired, "I'm going to keep my job. Even if the company closes, they'll offer me a job!"

That is success. Success begins in the heart. Success does not begin on the outside, and it is not measured by how many material possessions we have or how much influence we have on others. It begins inside, and it is measured by how much Word we have in our hearts.

The Word Is My Comfort

Even in troubled times, you can be successful when you remember the Word. Psalm 119 says:

> Remember the word unto thy servant, upon which thou hast caused me to hope. This is my comfort in my affliction: for thy word hath quickened me.

> PSALM 119:49,50

The psalmist's comfort in his affliction was the Word of God. He placed his hope in that Word, and it strengthened him and filled him with the confidence of God.

In the midst of your affliction, your troubled time, you shall find comfort in the Word of God. In the middle of all of the problems that surround you, you can open the Bible and begin to meditate on the Word. Your problems will be reduced to tiny situations when you put them next to God's Word, and that is when you will know true success.

Study Questions

1. What does it mean to cast away your confidence?

_____

_____

_____

_____

_____

2. How can a Christian delight in the Word of God?

_____

_____

_____

_____

_____

3. Describe a time when the Lord gave you enlightenment.
What do you need His wisdom about today?

_____

_____

_____

_____

_____

4. Why is daily confession important?

_____

_____

_____

_____

_____

5. In what areas do you want to see your life change? What can you do in order to begin finding success in that area?

_____

_____

_____

_____

Take a few minutes to write down the verses God has shown you that can help you keep your mind on Him.

_____

_____

_____

_____

Conclusion:
It's Only Temporary

The ultimate weapon against trouble is the knowledge that it is only temporary. No matter what the devil brings against us, it is subject to change! The Apostle Paul had more trouble during his ministry than most of us can even imagine. However, Paul was not troubled, because he knew the problems were only temporary. He knew he had a shield against trouble that would never fail him. That shield was the Word of God.

By reading Paul's letters, we can learn so much about walking in the confidence of God in the middle of trouble. In 2 Corinthians 4:8–10, for example, he gives us some insight into his success:

> *We are troubled on every side, yet not distressed; we are perplexed, but not in despair; persecuted, but not forsaken; cast down, but not destroyed; always bearing about in the body the dying of the Lord Jesus, that the life also of Jesus might be made manifest in our body.*

Paul offers even more specific direction to us in the following verses. When you look at these verses, remember that Jesus and the Word are one. Therefore, in order to clarify the application of these verses, I have inserted "the Word of God" where Paul writes "Jesus."

Look at verses 10, 11, and 16 this way:

> *Always bearing about in the body the dying of the Lord Jesus, that the life also of [the Word of God] might be made manifest in our bodies.*
>
> *For we which live are always delivered unto death for Jesus' sake, that the life also of [the Word of God] might be made manifest in our mortal flesh.*
>
> *For which cause we faint not; but though our outward man perish, yet the inward man is renewed day by day.*

For the cause of the life that is in the Word, Paul says we must not faint—give up, cave in, or quit. Verse 16 in *The Amplified Bible* says, "Therefore we do not become discouraged (utterly spiritless, exhausted, and wearied out through fear). Though our outer man is [progressively] decaying and wasting away, yet our inner self is being [progressively] renewed day after day."

Is trouble in your way? That's all right: When you are filling yourself to overflowing with the Word of God, your inward self is being renewed day by day. If you spent time in the Word yesterday, then when you got up this morning you had a renewed inward self. If you spend time in the Word today, then tomorrow you will have a renewed inward self. If you spend time in the Word tomorrow, then the next day you will have a renewed inward self.

The day that you do not allow the Word of God to renew your inward self is the day that you become susceptible to the trouble in this world. However, if you stay in the Word daily, you can continue to rise above your problems. Even when they seem enormous to the people around you, those problems will be nothing to you.

Look at Paul's attitude toward the terrible trouble that surrounded him. He said, "For our light affliction . . ." (2 Cor. 4:17). In context, we see that what Paul called *light affliction* was a shipwreck, being thrown in jail, and being beaten with a whip. Would you and I have this attitude toward such circumstances? If we set our hearts on the Word of God every day, as Paul did, we would!

Only Temporary

Not only did Paul call his trouble "light," but he said, "which is but for a moment. . . ." How long this moment was for him was irrelevant. No matter how long it was, Paul understood that it was only temporary. In verses 17–18 he writes:

> *For our light affliction, which is but for a moment, worketh for us a far more exceeding and eternal weight*

of glory; while we look not at the things which are seen,
but at the things which are not seen: for the things
which are seen are temporal; but the things which are
not seen are eternal.

Things "which are seen" are things that are perceived by the physical senses. Paul tells us that these things are "temporal." In other words, circumstances are *temporary.*

Can you remember a problem you had five years ago? Do you still have it, or is it gone? Most likely, there were problems nagging you five years ago that you can't even remember today, because that situation was subject to change.

Remember: Whatever you have been through and whatever you are going through is subject to change! It won't last forever! Therefore, you can laugh at the Devil because whatever problem he throws at you is subject to change. You need to tell him, "I know this is just temporary! This is going to change!"

Subject to Change!

Did the doctor give you a bad report about your body? *Don't get upset! It's just a temporary thing!* This too must pass! If everything else in your past is in your past, then this is going to go where all of that stuff is—in your past! It is subject to change!

Is your marriage suffering? The problems in your relationship are subject to change!

Did you lose your job? Your unemployment is temporary!

Do you have more bills than you have income? That deficit is soon to be history!

I don't care what the problem is—it is subject to change!

Stay in the Word, because your situation is subject to change. Do not allow a temporary situation to affect you. Only allow the Word to affect you.

Eternal Things

The Word of God is not temporary; it is eternal. Eternal things will affect temporary things. You may be presented with some difficult facts, but if they are not absolute Bible truths, they are temporary. Facts are temporary and can be changed by eternal Bible truth.

For example, the doctor may tell you that you have cancer. However, because that is not what the Word says, that is not the truth. Therefore, you can go to the truth of the Word and say, "By His stripes I am healed." That truth changes a fact! That eternal truth makes cancer temporary.

Do not be afraid of facts. They can only stay a little while anyway. Do not let facts convince you that the problem is powerful. Do not put confidence in the problem's ability, because it is just temporary. It has to go, and you do not have to go with it!

No matter what you are going through, it is temporary. It is only for a moment. Don't spend your time and energy focusing on a passing problem. Instead, set your mind and heart on the eternal truth of the Word of God.

Be Not Troubled

Although trouble comes, it does not have to overcome. You do not have to be troubled. You can walk in the confidence of God when you are resting on the Word of God. As a born-again child of God, as an heir of salvation, you are not of the system of this world. Therefore, you do not have to operate according to the system of this world. You can have peace, and you can walk in the confidence of God, because you can operate according to the system of God's Word!

Every time a problem arises, from this day on, I want you to remember our Savior's powerful words in John 16:33:

> *These things I have spoken unto you, that in me ye might have peace. In the world ye shall have tribulation: but be of good cheer; I have overcome the world.*

The next time a problem tries to steal your attention, remember: Jesus, the Word of God, has already overcome it. Hold on to that Word, pay attention to that Word, and your problems will disappear as God rewards you with the benefits of your salvation. Expect to walk in the confidence of God, because as you hold on to Jesus and His Word, together you will overcome the world.

Endnotes

Chapter 1

1. Strong, James H. "A Greek Dictionary of the New Testament," in *Strong's Exhaustive Concordance* (Nashville: Abingdon, 1890), 70.
2. ———. "Greek Dictionary of the New Testament," in *Strong's Exhaustive Concordance* (Nashville: Abingdon, 1890), 26.

Chapter 3

1. *The American Heritage Dictionary of the English Language* (New York: Houghton Mifflin, 1970), 141.
2. I am indebted to Charles Capps for these daily confessions, which I learned from his book *God's Creative Power Will Work for You*. The complete text of these confessions, with their Scripture references, can also be found in Charles Capps' *Faith and Confession* (Tulsa: Harrison House, 1987), 307–315.

About the Author

DR. CREFLO A. DOLLAR is the founder and senior pastor of World Changers Church International (WCCI) in College Park, Georgia, and World Changers Church-New York. With 20 years of experience in ministry, Dr. Dollar is committed to bringing the Good News of Jesus Christ to people all over the world, literally changing the world one person at a time.

A former educational therapist, Dr. Dollar received the vision for World Changers in 1986. He held the church's first worship service in the cafeteria of Kathleen Mitchell Elementary School in College Park with only eight people in attendance. Over the years the ministry grew rapidly, and the congregation moved from the cafeteria to a modest-sized chapel, adding a weekly radio broadcast and four services each Sunday. On December 24, 1995, WCCI moved into its present location, the 8,500–seat sanctuary known as the World Dome. At a cost of nearly $20 million, the World Dome was built without any bank financing. The construction of the World Dome is a testament to the miracle-working power of

God and remains a model of debt-freedom that ministries all over the world emulate.

A native of College Park, Dr. Dollar received his bachelor's degree in educational therapy from West Georgia College and was awarded a Doctor of Divinity degree from Oral Roberts University in 1998. He is the publisher of *CHANGE*, an international quarterly lifestyle magazine with over 100,000 subscribers that gives Christians the tools they need to experience total life prosperity. His award-winning *Changing Your World* television broadcast reaches nearly one billion homes in practically every country in the world. A much sought-after conference speaker and author, Dr. Dollar is known for his practical approach to the Bible and has encouraged thousands to pursue a personal relationship with God. Dr. Dollar and his wife, Taffi, have five children and live in Atlanta.

Books by Dr. Creflo A. Dollar

In the Presence of God
Live Without Fear
Not Guilty
Love, Live, and Enjoy Life
Breaking Out of Trouble
Walking in the Confidence of God in Troubled Times